HORRIBLE SCIENCE

ANNUAL 2012

THIS BOOK
BELONGS TO:

_____

_____

SCHOLASTIC

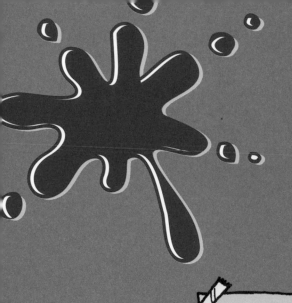

DEAR READER...

Welcome to your
HORRIBLE SCIENCE 2012 annual -
a buzzing, barfing book of scientific
brilliance that zips from nuke to
(pizza) puke! Have a spin at making a
whizzing water turbine, discover the
deafening deal behind noise and then
squeeze in at the front of a crazy
concert. Catch some amazing rays in
the park and then make light go bendy!
Bend your brains with some freaky
illusions - you won't believe your
eyeballs... that is, when you've
finished EATING them. It's enough to
make a science teacher go nuclear!

CONTENTS

BURNING ISSUES

Fearsome fuels have energy to burn. They keep your television glowing, your car rolling and your mushy peas boiling over, but little by little they are poisoning the world. Perhaps our only hope is to find a new super-fuel…

IN THE OXFORDSHIRE COUNTRYSIDE, THERE IS AN EXPERIMENTAL FACILITY CALLED J.E.T. HERE, SCIENTISTS ARE TRYING TO MASTER AN AMAZING NEW WAY OF MAKING ENERGY CALLED NUCLEAR FUSION…

LET'S GIVE IT ANOTHER WHIRL, BOB

CAN'T A MAN EAT A DOUGHNUT IN PEACE?

FUSION POWER COULD GIVE US ENDLESS ENERGY WITHOUT ANY MESS, BUT SO FAR IT'S PROVED A LITTLE TRICKY TO CONTROL…

CRACKLE!

SPARK!

YIKES!

ERM… A BIT LESS POWER NEXT TIME…

…SO IT'S STILL A FUEL FOR THE FUTURE.

MANKIND HAS ALWAYS TRIED TO FIND BETTER FUELS. FIRST WE BURNT WOOD AND COAL… THEN GAS, OIL AND PETROL. NUCLEAR MATERIALS WERE ADDED TO THIS LIST IN THE 20TH CENTURY.

wood   coal   gas   oil   petrol   nuclear

THE FUELISH STORY ALL GOT GOING WHEN SOME ANCIENT HUMANS DISCOVERED FIRE, WHICH HELPED TO FUEL SOME BIG LEAPS FORWARD, SUCH AS...

COOKING...

DON'T THINK MUCH OF THIS FANCY MODERN CUISINE

— wood fuel

GLASS-BLOWING...

OH BLOW!

charcoal fuel

...AND SMELTING (MAKING METAL FROM ORE).

'S MELTING

charcoal fuel

PEOPLE MADE FIRES OUT OF WOOD, CHARCOAL AND PEAT... AND WHEN THAT WAS SCARCE, STRAW MIXED WITH COWPATS! YUCK!

THAT'S DUNG IT!

KAF KAF

WHAT I'D DO FOR SMOKELESS FUEL

ANIMAL FAT WAS USED IN OIL LAMPS, BUT BY ABOUT 200 BC THE CHINESE WERE USING OIL. THE PROBLEM WAS, THE SMOKE WAS REALLY STINKY!

THIS IS WORSE THAN THE COWPAT!

SO IT DIDN'T CATCH ON... YET.

LUCKILY, HUMANS DISCOVERED COAL. THIS DARK CRUMBLY ROCK IS MADE OUT OF MILLIONS OF FOSSILIZED PLANTS, SO IT'S CALLED A FOSSIL FUEL.

ONE NIGHT IN THE LATE 17TH CENTURY, THOMAS SAVERY LOBBED HIS WINE BOTTLE ONTO HIS COAL FIRE. THE DRUNKEN DABBLER NOTICED THE STEAM RUSHING OUT OF THE BOTTLE'S NECK.

...I'M SHTOOPID AN' USHELESSH AT SCHIENCE... HANG ON A MINUTE...

SAVERY REALIZED THAT THERE WAS ENERGY IN THE STEAM AND INVENTED THE FIRST COAL-FIRED STEAM ENGINES. THEY WERE IMPROVED UPON AND SOON USED FOR EVERYTHING...

I PREFERRED THINGS THE WAY THEY WERE

HOWL! MY MONEY'S GONE UP IN SMOKE!

SOOTS YOU!

IT'S-TEAM EFFORT

BRIGHT SPARK AND SCOTTISH SCIENTIST WILLIAM MURDOCK FOUND OUT HOW TO GET GAS FROM COAL AND IN 1792, INVENTED THE FIRST GAS LIGHT.

YOU LIGHT UP MY WORLD!

FUEL WAS NOW THE BURNING ISSUE AND SCIENTISTS BEGAN TO WONDER WHERE THE HUMAN BODY GOT ITS ENERGY FROM...

StINK OR STEAM

Fired with enthusiasm, energy fanatics have come up with many foul, false and fantastic ideas about fuel over the years...

Phosphorus Pee

In the 1800s, British scientist John Walker and later Swedish inventor John Lundstrum helped invent the matches we still use today. But the burning fuel in matches – phosphorus – was discovered in 1669 in Hamburg, Germany, by nutty scientist Hennig Brandt. In his stinking laboratory he discovered that glowing buckets of rotting wee contained phosphorous. He boiled it and dried it into a white powder!

Brandt tried to keep this secret but he got drunk on the idea and two awful alchemists, named Krafft and Kunckel, stole his process and made a fortune. Bitter Brandt was a bit pee-ved!

Getting Steamed Up

Steam was one of the first forms of energy ever discovered, and it's driven many boats, trains and other machines since. Steam was originally discovered during the **Roman Empire**, but the **Romans** were more interested in slave power than steam power!

One of the first steam-powered inventions was created by **Hero of Alexandria**. Here's how it might have been advertized in the Horrible Science of the day.

No one knows what the revolving ball was for – other than being a strange toy – but smart **Hero** also invented steam-powered doors that closed automatically and a windmill-powered organ. Now that's what you call a real hero!

Big Banger

William Murdock became famous for building steam engines that ran on the road like cars. In 1801, Murdock's pal, inventor Richard Trevithick (1771-1833), built his own steam carriage and took it for a spin. It broke down, but the inventor managed to fix it and went to the pub to celebrate. Unfortunately, he left the fire on – the boiler boiled dry and the engine exploded!

POWERFUEL POTENTIAL

Oil, gas and coal aren't the only available fuels. Here are a few powerful ideas to fuel your imagination. Whether you're into subterranean hot water or rotting poo in space, read on...

Fossil fuels will run out some day. Before that happens, there's another problem: when burned, they produce lots of carbon dioxide – a gas that's making the world's climate go wrong. If we want to keep watching TV, it's a good idea to find new ways of making energy.

Going nuclear

Some scientists believe the answer is to think super small – smaller than atoms – and go nuclear. Nuclear power stations don't pump fumes into the air, but they do create radioactive waste. Radioactive things have atoms which are decaying – giving off neutrons, some of the teeny tiny things they're made of. The neutrons can cause serious damage to the atoms around them – including the atoms that make up you and me. This is why radioactivity can be dangerous.

Dead Disgusting

Some revolting materials have been used as fuel:
• In the year 2000 some UK power stations made electricity from burning the remains of dead, diseased cows.
• A man in Manchester, England, ran his car on oil from the local chip shop that had been changed chemically into diesel oil. He could have run it on oranges but then he'd have run out of juice, ha ha!
• French cement companies have burnt used nappies to heat their cement-making kilns.

POOH! THAT REALLY STINKS

BURN!

Cough! SPLUTTER!

OUI! IT SURE DOES

NUCLEAR FACT FILE

NAME: Nuclear Power

THE BASIC FACTS:
1. Atoms are held together by huge forces. So if the atoms are torn apart, the energy of these forces is released, together with deadly radioactive rays that can kill by blistering the skin and destroying the lining of the guts.

2. One kilogram of uranium atoms can release enough energy to lift 200 million elephants one metre into the air.

WE'RE HERE FOR THE URANIUM EXPERIMENT

WAY OUT →

3. In nuclear power stations the heat energy from splitting atoms boils water, creating steam that drives turbines and makes electricity.

HORRIBLE DETAILS:
1. At Three Mile Island in the USA in 1979, and at Chernobyl in the Ukraine in 1986, nuclear power stations went out of control and released radioactive gas and dust.

LEAK! LEAK! LEAK! LEAK!

2. Power stations create radioactive waste that can stay dangerous for tens of thousands of years.

Many happy returns

We need to keep looking for cleaner energies. The wind, waves, tides and Sun are already used to create energy. These natural types of energy are called 'renewable' because there's always more of them. You've probably heard of them. However, deep within the Earth there's another type of renewable energy that's less well-known. Here's how YOU can tap into it...

How To Build Your Own Geothermal Power Station

INTRODUCTION

A geothermal power station taps into very hot rock thousands of metres under your feet to release heat energy. This actually makes it possible to grow bananas in Iceland (in greenhouses). So why not have a bash at building your own geothermal power station?

- No more nasty energy bills
- Piping hot water for ever
- No cost except for the few hundred million that you will spend building your own power station

HEAT!

hot rock

Planet Earth

WHAT YOU WILL NEED

two drill rigs

heavy lifting gear, bulldozers and building materials

several kilometres of pipes

very rich understanding parents

an Olympic-sized swimming pool or private lake

INSTRUCTIONS

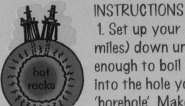

hot rocks

house   pipes

1. Set up your rigs and drill 7km (4.2 miles) down until you reach rocks hot enough to boil water. Push a pipe down into the hole you drill. You've made a 'borehole'. Make another one!

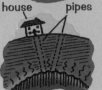

2. Link up the pipes from your second borehole with your house's hot water system. Your relatives may want their house to be plumbed in too!

pool

3. Now for the FUN! Link the pipes from your first borehole to the swimming pool and open the valve so water rushes down the hole.

boiling water

4. Superheated hot water will rush up the second borehole and into your hot water system!

WARNING: adjust the pressure of your radiators or they may explode!

THE SMALL PRINT

If molten rock oozes from your boreholes you've created a volcano that could bury your neighbourhood under loads of red-hot lava.

whoops!

Sun and stink power

We might discover a new kind of power. Could these be news stories from the future…?

IT WORKS!

Super-Sun Satellite Soars

Scientists are thrilled at the success of a giant satellite going around the Sun. It picks up power and beams it to Earth as microwave rays.

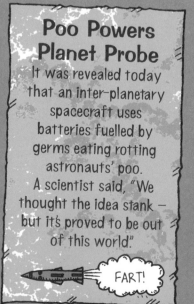

Poo Powers Planet Probe

It was revealed today that an inter-planetary spacecraft uses batteries fuelled by germs eating rotting astronauts' poo. A scientist said, "We thought the idea stank – but it's proved to be out of this world."

FART!

Pants ideas

Some energy ideas are load of hot baloney. Foolish folk who believe UFOs are alien spacecraft have suggested that they work by some kind of anti-gravity force. This idea isn't new – in 1878, the inventor Thomas Edison wanted to make anti-gravity underwear that floated around in mid-air!

FREAKY FISSION

Q: What is a nuclear scientist's favourite meal?

A: Fission chips! But just what is 'fission'? It's when the core of an atom is split in two, that's what! Cracking!

1. At the heart of a nuclear power station is the reactor, a thick steel and concrete container crammed full of uranium fuel rods (**1a**). These are the power source.

2. Inside the reactor, everything is powered by neutrons (new-trons). These tiny, whizzing particles make up part of the centre of an atom, called the nucleus. When the nucleus of the uranium atom gets hit by a neutron, it splits in two and releases two more neutrons. These can then split two other uranium nuclei, and so very quickly a 'chain reaction' has been started. If the chain reaction isn't controlled, it explodes – in fact, it would be a nuclear bomb, which would certainly make things go off with a bang! So control rods made of graphite (that's the stuff in your pencil lead) are lowered into the reactor to mop up excess neutrons and slow the reaction down (**2a**).

3. Nuclear fission gives off loads of heat in milliseconds. The heat goes into surrounding water.

4. This boiling water travels in pipes through a steam generator, where it heats more cold water.

5. As the water becomes hot it turns to steam. Water molecules (groups of atoms) (**5a**) rush out of the steam generator along pipes to the turbine.

6. The high-pressure steam pushes blades inside the turbine and makes them rotate (go round).

7. The rotating turbine powers a generator which makes electricity.

8. As the steam cools and becomes water again, it drops into the condenser (**8a**) where it is pumped back to the steam generator.

9. Used uranium is horribly hazardous and stays harmful for thousands of years. It must be buried underground in giant concrete ponds or deep bunkers (**9a**).

MAKE YOUR OWN
WATER TURBINE

You can harness the energy that's in running water by using a machine called a 'water turbine'. Why not make one – then see a nuclear reaction on the kitchen table!

You will need:
- an empty milk or soup carton (about 1/2 litre)
- cotton or thread (not string)
- a corkscrew
- masking tape
- a large jug of water

1 Take your carton (empty and washed, of course!) and carefully use the corkscrew to make a small clean hole in each of the four bottom corners as shown. Be careful with the end of the corkscrew – it's very sharp!

2 Make another hole in the top of the carton, thread some cotton through it and tie a knot. Also open the carton so water can go in.

3 Now firmly seal over each of the four holes, using pieces of masking tape, leaving some tape over the edge of the carton so you can remove it easily later.

4 Hang up the carton outside, tying the cotton to a tree branch or washing line. Avoid doing this experiment in your house or everything might get wet!

5 Now you're ready. Gently pour some water into the carton until it's nearly full. Now uncover one of the holes. Stand back a bit! The water spurts out and the carton begins to spin on the cotton...

6 Quickly uncover the hole from the opposite corner, and then try with three, then four holes. Refill with more water if necessary. The more holes uncovered, the more powerfully your turbine will spin!

You will need:
- 15 dominoes
- a flat, solid table or floor surface
- a ruler

Make a nuclear chain reaction!

1 Arrange 15 dominoes like this. Think of the dominoes as uranium atoms.

2 Now the exciting bit! Push over the first domino and watch as each domino hits two more, and so on, causing a chain reaction. That's nuclear power!

3 Arrange five dominoes in a straight line, and hold a ruler between the fourth and fifth domino.

4 Push one end of the five dominoes. The ruler stops the last one toppling. Like a control rod in a nuclear power station, the ruler has controlled the effect.

15

PUZZLES

GEIGER COUNTER

Imagine you have a super-sensitive Geiger counter (an instrument which responds to radioactivity by making loud clicks – the more radioactivity, the faster the clicks). Which would just set it off a bit, and which would make it click like a pair of nuclear-powered castanets?

1. smoke alarm
7. real Cornish rock
2. fire alarm
3. X-ray
5. helium balloon
10. neon tube
9. fossil paperweight
4. 'heavy' hydrogen
8. mobile phone
6. heart pacemaker

WHICH SWITCH?

A nuclear reactor's fuel rods are overheating! It's up to you to flick the correct switch to lower the rods back into the water. But which is the right switch?

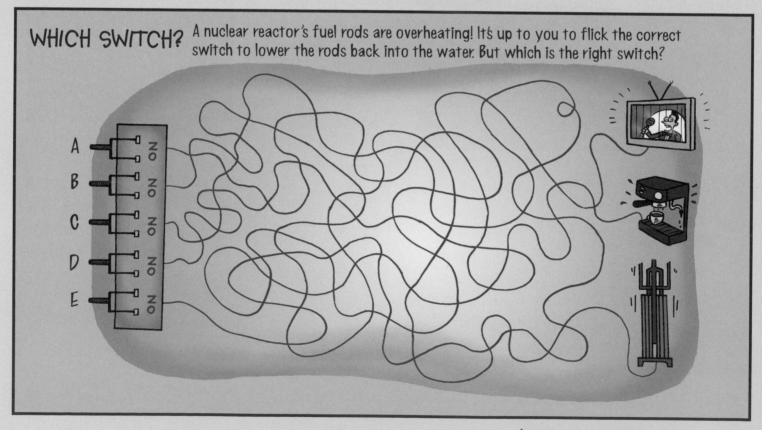

A
B
C
D
E

Answers on page 60.

DISGUSTING DIET

Just like a car needs petrol, you need food. Without it, you'd come to a stop! But today, there's just so much of it around, how do you know which will keep you running like a limo rather than spluttering like a junkheap? Read on...

There's a lot more to food than meets the eye. There are loads of vital ingredients that you must have in your daily diet. To find out more we persuaded our private investigator, MI Gutzache, to sneak into the school kitchens to collect samples...

Gutzache investigates

It was time for the protective suit. And I insisted on a gas mask... these particular samples smelled ancient. I figured they could be emetic (that means something that makes you sick as a dog)!

Sample 1 – School Dinner Potato

This sad potato was about to be boiled, but was still a healthy specimen. This is what I found hiding in it:

- One slug*
- 81% water
- 0.4% protein
- 16% carbohydrate (in the form of starch)
- 0.1% fat
- 0.8% fibre
- 0.7% vitamins
- 1% minerals

HI!

NOTES
The slug had no complaints

* The slug also contained these ingredients but in different amounts. At least this time it didn't get cooked with the potato!

Sample 2 – School Dinner Chips

The chips were cold, super greasy and oozing with fat. Fat is a funny thing; some types can gunk up your insides, while others can be good for you.

Sample 3 – Jam Pudding

This pud is oozing with sticky sugar. Sugars give your body energy – but too much of this type can make you fatter than an extra-thick chip.

NOTES
Just looking at it gave me toothache

Sample 4 – Mashed Swede

Hidden in this weird lump of orange vegetable I found a tasteless food chemical called starch – a type of carbohydrate, the same as in potato. It's made of sugar chemicals joined in a chain. Inside your muscles enzymes can rip these sugars apart and free the energy to help your body move.

Sample 5 – Smelly Cheese

NOTES
Relieved to find the smell wasn't coming from my socks

GHASTLY PONG

Cheese is 25% protein – your body uses this to build muscles. Your body is 20% protein but you don't need to eat tonnes of it. If you're 12 years old you need about 55 grams of protein a day. Protein also hangs out in milk, fish, meat, beans and nuts.

I've sketched some useful sources of protein

SICKENING SCOFFING

'Competitive eating' is a crazy sort of game in which speedy-greedy guts scoff as much as they can in a short time! It's the worst possible way to eat - so, in a disgusting way, it tells us a lot about how guzzling works. We've sent in a team of belly boffins to see how speed scoffers do it...

1. Half the knack of speed eating is being quick and skilful at folding food up (useful for hot dogs) or pulling food apart (essential for chicken wings – chicken bones can be fatal!) before it's shovelled down.

2. Rapidly filling your stomach with lots of barely chewed food often creates HEARTBURN. Despite the name, this has got nothing to do with your heart! The burning feeling is caused by acidic stomach juices that are splashing up the gullet (2a).

3. Rushing down food and being stressed makes you swallow air. This causes cramps and gut aches. Just proves you should always eat slowly and chew your food!

4. Why do people do this? For trophies... and cash prizes! People will do all sorts of stupid things for cash prizes – it's a scientifically proven fact!

5. Adults' stomachs have a volume of about one litre. Competitive eaters practise stretching their bellies to four litres or more by filling themselves with water or a low-calorie food such as cabbage. The belly can stretch like this because its folds – rugae – can open out (5a). HORRIBLE SCIENCE WARNING: Drinking stupid amounts of water is dangerous.

6. Speed-eaters' brains seem to be able to ignore signals of discomfort from their stomachs (6a). If scientists can find out how they do it, they might be able to help NORMAL eaters who suffer from stomach pain (dyspepsia).

7. Speed-eating can make you fart terribly... and give you diarrhoea.

8. The 'gag' reflex is another nerve impulse that speed eaters can 'override' – sometimes! So NEVER eat like a speed eater unless you really want to be sick. Competitive eaters puke a lot.

9. You are allowed to vomit in speed eating competitions... as long as none of it leaves your mouth. YUCK!! But this is doubly horrid, as vomiting does a lot of harm – splashing the teeth with acid that erodes the enamel (9a).

10. All speed eaters eventually 'hit the wall' – which means they reach a point where the brain says "NO MORE!" You might get this after a double helping of Christmas dinner. It's just as well that the body shuts down like this. Eating HUGE amounts of anything puts a terrible strain on your heart, liver and kidneys (10a).

SPLASH AND BURN

GROSS FOOD FACTORY

You might be amazed at how much of the food we eat is processed like a product from a factory. This meal machine takes it to a new nauseating level!

1. The first thing on the menu is pizza, which needs tomato purée. Our tomatoes aren't grown in soil. How do they grow, you say? Well...

2. They're grown 'hydroponically'. This means the plants' roots grow in a clean substance – such as plastic granules, volcanic minerals or fleece – where they're fed with nutrient-packed water (**2a**). (This is how 65% of all tomatoes sold in British supermarkets are grown.) The water is recycled and sterilized with ultra-violet light.

3. Fancy a shake? That's just milk and fruit, right? WRONG! This one has over 40 ingredients. The milk's not all that it seems, either. Of course, it comes from a cow in the beginning (**3a**) – but then the milk gets taken apart and re-built. It gets spray-dried (**3b**) and then water is added (**3c**). To keep those calories low (you'd rather have low calories than real food, wouldn't you?), we use a sweetener made from amino acids. And get this – there's not a single strawberry in there. It's all artificial flavours. To make sure the mix tastes of something we add some flavour enhancers (some amyl acetate for a banana taste, too)... and some more sweeteners... and a load of sugar! Thickeners make it gloopy... and stabilizers stop it going off.

4. For our fritters and pizza topping we use the nation's favourite, 'HAMP' – chopped ham with pork. How's it made? Simple! Pig in, kill pig, squeeze pork, chop ham (bum meat) (**4a**), grind, add water, sugar, salt, sodium nitrate (keeps it pink and prevents poisonous bacteria from growing) (**4b**), mix in vacuum (**4c**), put in tin, seal, cook in hot water (**4d**). Bingo – pink tinned pig!

5. Can't be bothered to boil and mash potatoes? Let the factory take the strain and make SPUDGE! After all, it's still made from potatoes that once grew in a field. Okay, so they get steam-washed, steam- and abrasion-peeled, sliced, pre-cooked, cooled, cooked again, dried, flaked then powdered and packaged (**5a**), losing a lot of goodness in the process. But... how does it all taste? Sorry, you've gone a bit green... feeling sick? Better not turn to page 24 then...

CHOMP!

EDIBLE EYEBALLS

Fancy cooking up something that's as delicious as it is revolting? How about crunchy chocolate eyeballs?

You will need:
- 25g Rice Krispies
- 75g milk chocolate
- 8 tbsp icing sugar
- giant Smarties
- black writing icing
- clingfilm
- saucepan
- bowl to fit over saucepan
- mixing bowl
- mixing spoon
- teaspoon

HORRIBLE HEALTH WARNING!
COOKING CAN BE DANGEROUS.
MAKE SURE YOU GET AN ADULT TO HELP
WITH THE PANEL MARKED WITH THIS SIGN.

1 Break up the chocolate and melt it in a bowl over a saucepan of boiling water. Mix the Rice Krispies into the melted chocolate and leave to cool.

MELT

POUR

TWIST!

2 Cut small squares of clingfilm and put a heaped teaspoonful of the mix on to each square. Shape into a ball, twist the ends together to secure and leave in the fridge to harden.

SPLODGE!

3 Put the icing sugar in a bowl and mix with warm water to make a thick paste. When cool, remove the clingfilm and coat the eyeballs with the icing.

GRRRR!

4 Stick a Smartie on to each eyeball and add a large black dot of writing icing as a pupil.

PUZZLES

BE A SCOFFIN' BOFFIN

Chefs aren't the only people who enjoy working with food. Scientists have done some mouth-watering experiments. Can you predict the results of these?

1. In the 1970s, a group of American scientists went to a party and watched people eating. The overweight people ate more than the thinner people. The scientists quickly grabbed the food and took it to another room. What happened next?

a) The overweight people went into the next room to get the food.
b) The overweight people wouldn't move. The thinner people went and helped themselves.
c) A fight broke out and the scientists were chucked out for spoiling the party.

EGG-SEPTIONAL

Eggs are all-round (or should that be all-oval) good food. But if you fall foul of the bacteria called salmonella (sal-mon-ella) that some carry, you'll be egg-stremely ill. Find out how much you know about eggs with this egg-scrutiating quiz...

1. Dyed or decorated eggs are always safe to eat.
TRUE/FALSE

2. Eggshell colour affects both an egg's taste and its nutritional quality.
TRUE/FALSE

3. Egg white contains no fat.
TRUE/FALSE

4. The best way to cook an egg to kill off any bacteria is:
a) poaching. **b)** hard boiling.
c) frying. **d)** scrambling.
e) all of these.

5. All eggs are pasteurized (heated to get rid of all bacteria).
TRUE/FALSE

6. You can tell an egg is rotten if:
a) it floats in water.
b) it pongs when opened.
c) its white is cloudy.
b) all of these.

Who said science is horrible?

SCRUMMY! YUMMY!

You're invited to a food party – eat as much as you like, but watch out for people in white coats trying to snatch the food away from you!

---

2. In the 1970s, more American scientists asked a group of people to sample a selection of yummy ice creams after first slurping down a rich, sweet, milk shake. What did they find?
a) People who were trying to lose weight ate more ice cream.
b) People who were trying to lose weight ate less ice cream.
c) Everyone scoffed as much as they could because the food was free, then threw up everywhere.

WHATEVER COULD IT BE?

Cross out nine letters so that the remaining letters, without altering their sequence, spell a familiar fun-to-eat, full-of-goodness fruit.

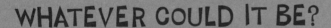

BSAINXLEATNTEAR

OK – THAT'S THE MILK SHAKE AND ICE CREAM TEST, NOW WE MOVE ON TO THE FISHPASTE EXPERIMENT...

Answers on page 60.

PUKEY PIZZA

Found an old slice of pizza or a doughnut lurking forgotten in a corner – a lip-smacking, tasty bonus snack for you? Well, before you tuck in, read on...

1. Norman's had a slice of luck – he's found the missing piece of 'Good King Wenceslas Christmas Special' pizza (deep-pan, crisp and even – geddit?!) It's still in its box and just look at all that topping. Mmm, smells... er... interesting. There are even extra mushrooms. Munch! Hey, hang on, it didn't have fungi on it last week... and that green stuff isn't spinach!

2. The foul pizza's toxins react with Norman's body. He starts to feel very poorly. That's an essential part of the body's defence plan – if he didn't feel ill there'd be no limit to the damage the toxins could do. They irritate his stomach lining. He feels sick.

3. No one enjoys up-chucking but it's a brilliant way of emptying your stomach – fast. (But never try to make yourself sick!) In this case it gets rid of those naughty poisons.

4. Even so, Norm's gut lining has already absorbed poison and it now circulates in his bloodstream. He feels hot, shivery and wobbly-kneed. His pores enlarge to let sweat (and some poison) out, but it's still not enough.

5. Down in the engine room of his body, there's a right rumpus going on. His kidneys work overtime extracting any water-soluble poisons that can be passed out in his urine. Meanwhile, his liver filters out the non-water-soluble stuff **(5a)**. Its enzymes **(5b)** first absorb the toxins, making them less harmful, and then lead them away to join other processed matter, such as bile from the gall bladder, in his colon. Then they go to the final resting place for all good poisons...

6. The lav! (He'll survive!)

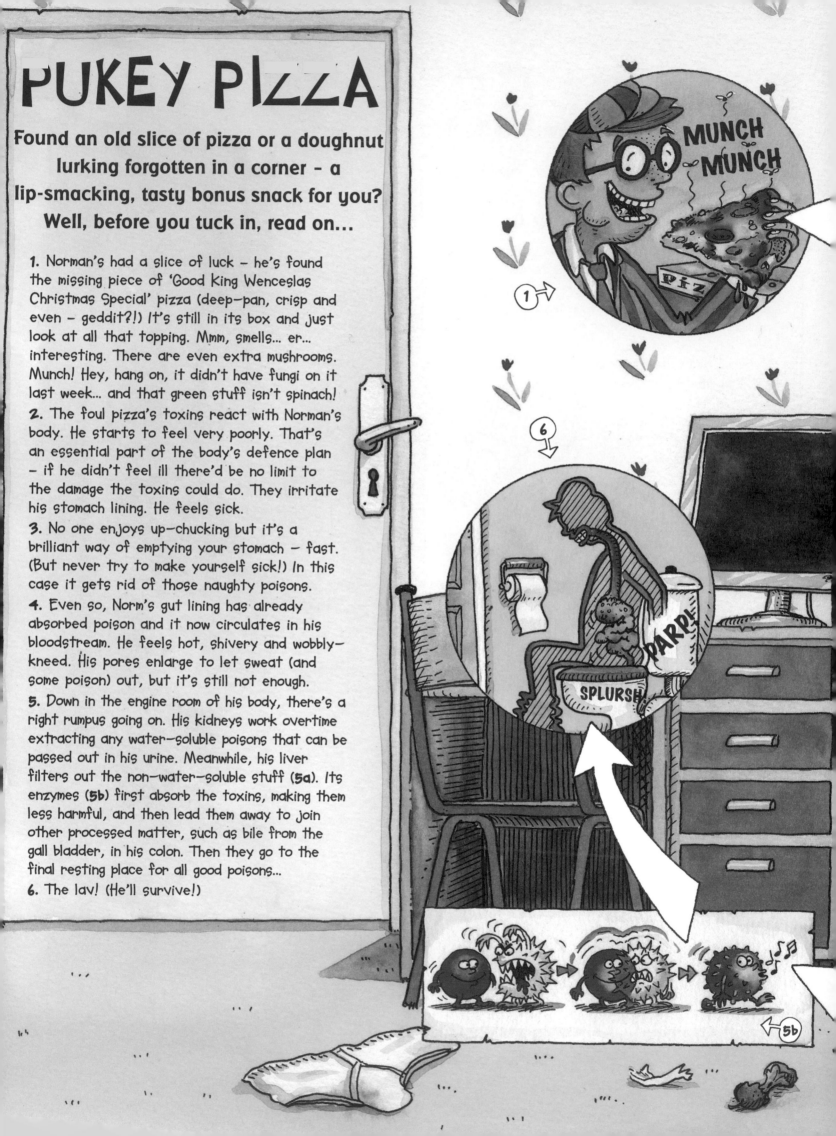

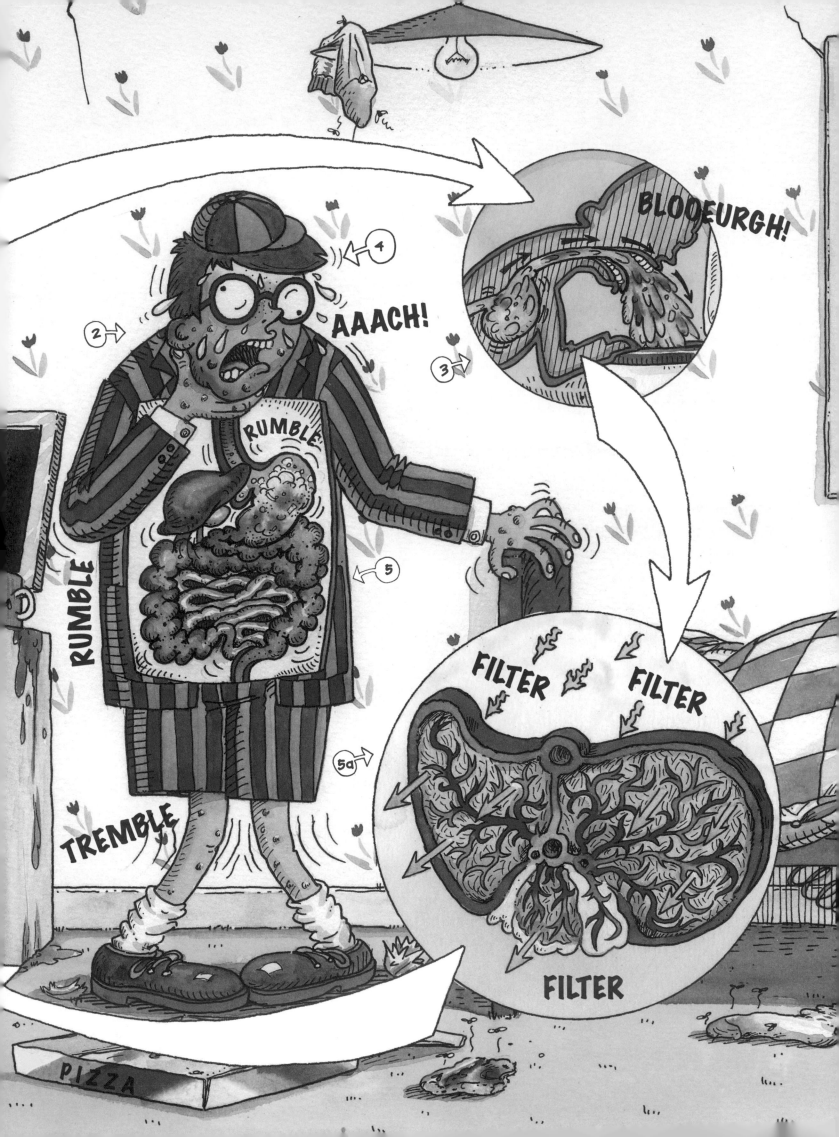

SHATTERING SOUNDS

A single note can shatter glass and make your eyeballs shiver in their sockets. Other sounds will make you run for the loo! Sounds unlikely? Read on...

The younger you are, the LOUDER you are. Babies love making noise and so do kids. And teenagers think that really loud music is brilliant!

TURN THAT THING OFF!

But as people grow older they change. They settle down and quieten down. Your parents no longer think LOUD is good. They think that anything LOUD sounds dreadful. Especially loud sounds made by YOU!

WILL YOU KIDS PLEASE BE QUIET!

ONLY IF YOU STOP SHOUTING AT US!

Dead Disgusting

In 1997 it was reported that US military bases in Britain were to be defended by powerful sound guns. Sounds waves from these machines would make any intruder's intestines vibrate so much they'd need to find a toilet in a hurry!

DON'T SUPPOSE YOU COULD LEND ME A CLEAN PAIR OF PANTS?

SOUNDS DREADFUL FACT FILE

NAME: Sound

THE BASIC FACTS: What we call 'sound' is really a wobbling (called a vibration) of tiny molecules in the air. This causes tiny changes in pressure which we detect through our eardrums.

COME ON! IT'S THE WRONG TIME OF YEAR FOR AVALANCHES... WHOOPS, SORRY!

THE HORRIBLE DETAILS: The force of a loud sound, such as a scream, can set off avalanches. In the winter of 1950–51, more than 240 people were buried alive by huge masses of snow crashing down mountainsides in Switzerland.

Sounding off

Scientists have their very own language to describe sounds. Here's your chance to sound off and amaze your friends and silence your teachers...

1. Amplitude

Amplitude (am-plee-tewd) means how loud a sound is. Stronger, taller sound waves mean louder sounds, or greater amplitude. The word 'amplitude' comes from 'ample', which also means BIG. Got that?

high amplitude sound waves (big sound = big sound wave)

ample scientist

CHEW

SCOFF

GOBBLE

MUNCH

ample dinner

2. Frequency

Frequency means the number of vibrations per second that make up a sound. These can be incredibly fast. For example, a bat squeak is a fantastic 200,000 vibrations per second. The higher the frequency, the higher the sound, which is why bats squeak rather than growl.

Frequency is measured in Hertz (say hurts). So higher frequency hurts more… erm… makes more Hertz. One Hertz (Hz) is one vibration per second. Your amazingly alert ears can pick up sounds from about 25Hz to 20,000Hz.

High-frequency sounds include…

• A MOUSE SQUEAKING.

SQUEEEEEEEAK!

SQUEAK!

• A HUMAN SQUEAKING AFTER SEEING THE MOUSE.

Low-frequency sounds include…

• A BEAR GROWLING.

GROWL!

GROWL!

• YOUR DAD GROWLING IN THE MORNING.

tuning fork

music teacher keeping in tune in the music room

gardening fork

music teacher keeping in tune in the garden

3. Tones

A tone is a sound with just one frequency (most sounds are 'polyphonic' – polly-fon-ick – with lots mixed together). You can make a tone by hitting a special tool called a tuning fork on a smooth surface.

4. Resonance

Resonance (rez-o-nance) is when vibrations hit an object at a certain frequency and make it wobble, too. The vibrations get stronger and stronger, making the sound louder and louder – until it's deafening.

resonating bell

resonating scientist

CLANG!

DARE YOU DISCOVER…
why shells sound like the sea?

You will need:
A fairly large seashell shaped like this:

All you do is:
Put the open end of the shell to your ear and listen. What is causing those eerie sound effects?

1. The ghostly echoes of the sea.
2. It's the sounds around you resonating in the shell.
3. Faint sounds stored by chemical structures in the shell are released by the heat of your body.

Answer on page 60.

ROTTEN RACKETS

Do you enjoy escaping from science homework by listening to music? Do you download tracks to turn your back on maths? If so, brace yourself – you're about to read something that will change the way you think about music forever!

THE BAD NEWS IS THAT FROM THE MINUTE IT'S MADE TO THE SECOND IT'S REPLAYED, MUSIC IS MATHS MADE BY SCIENCE!

MUSIC IS MATHS?! NO, THAT'S HORRIBLE! I DON'T WANNA HEAR IT!

GOOD, BECAUSE NEITHER DO I!

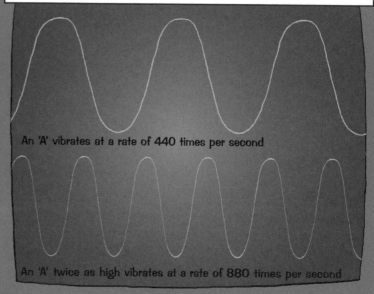

IT'S TRUE – THE DIFFERENCE BETWEEN NOTES IS ALL ABOUT MATHS. THE NOTE 'A' NEAR THE MIDDLE OF A PIANO'S KEYBOARD IS A WAVE THAT VIBRATES 440 TIMES PER SECOND. AN 'A' THAT'S TWICE AS HIGH HAS DOUBLE THIS 'FREQUENCY'.

An 'A' vibrates at a rate of 440 times per second

An 'A' twice as high vibrates at a rate of 880 times per second

AND EVERY INSTRUMENT HAS BEEN IMPROVED THROUGH SCIENCE. FOR EXAMPLE, EARLY PIPE ORGANS WERE POWERED BY A PUMP THAT WAS SO WHEEZY THE ORGAN COULD ONLY MANAGE A FEW NOTES, QUITE WIDE APART. THE INVENTION OF BETTER PUMPS MEANT MORE CONTROL, SO MORE NOTES!

MOAN PUFF WHEEZE

SIX NOTES?! HORRIBLE MODERN RACKET!

IT WAS THE SAME WITH BRASS INSTRUMENTS (TRUMPETS, HORNS, TUBAS). THEY COULDN'T PLAY TOGETHER BECAUSE RUBBISH ENGINEERING MEANT THEY WERE OUT OF TUNE!

OH DEAR, HE'S GETTING A BIT BRASSED OFF!

PRECISION ENGINEERING IN THE 19TH CENTURY MEANT THE INSTRUMENTS' VALVES WORKED BETTER – AND SO THEY COULD ALL PLAY TOGETHER AS A BRASS SECTION.

TECHNOLOGY CHANGES THE WAY MUSIC IS MADE. THE INVENTION OF MICROPHONES MEANT THAT VOICES COULD BE AMPLIFIED (MADE LOUDER) SO SINGERS DIDN'T HAVE TO WAIL AT THE TOP OF THEIR VOICES. IT TOOK A WHILE FOR PEOPLE TO GET THE HANG OF THIS...

PROBABLY THE MOST POPULAR AMPLIFIED INSTRUMENT TODAY IS THE ELECTRIC GUITAR. THE FIRST ONE WAS INVENTED IN 1931 AND WAS NICKNAMED THE 'FRYING PAN'!

IN THE 1920s A BRAINY INVENTOR CALLED LEO THEREMIN MADE AN INSTRUMENT THAT REALLY GOT ELECTRONIC MUSIC GOING. IT WAS PLAYED BY WAVING YOUR ARMS ABOUT!

AMAZINGLY, THEREMIN WAS ALSO A RUSSIAN SPY, AND HE INVENTED THE FIRST BUGS FOR RUSSIA.

IN THE 1970s AND '80s, SYNTHESIZERS AND OTHER ELECTRONIC INSTRUMENTS WERE ALL THE RAGE. DRUM MACHINES WERE INVENTED TO TAKE THE PLACE OF DRUMMERS. THE MACHINES NEVER RAN OUT OF ENERGY AND THEY STAYED IN TIME!

IN THE 1980s THERE WAS A REAL SCIENTIFIC BREAKTHROUGH – THE INVENTION OF A COMPUTER LANGUAGE CALLED 'MIDI' – 'MUSICAL INSTRUMENT DIGITAL INTERFACE'. NOW ELECTRONIC INSTRUMENTS COULD COMMUNICATE WITH EACH OTHER.

THE WAY WE PLAY BACK MUSIC ALL DEPENDS ON THE SCIENCE OF OUR TIME. IN THE EARLY 20TH CENTURY, PIANOLAS WERE THE COOL THING. THEY USED PNEUMATIC POWER. TO PLAY MUSIC, YOU PUT A ROLL OF PERFORATED PAPER IN IT. HOLES IN THE PAPER TOLD THE PNEUMATICS WHEN TO PLAY THE KEYS. THE PIANO PLAYED ITSELF!

TROUBLE WAS, PLAYBACK PIANOS WEREN'T EXACTLY PORTABLE!

I LIKE A LITTLE LIGHT PIANO MUSIC AS I WALK!

TINKLE PLONK BONG

COULD BE WORSE, I SUPPOSE - HE COULD LIKE HEAVY METAL!

AFTER WAX CYLINDERS, THE FIRST TRULY POPULAR MASS-PRODUCED MUSIC PLAYER WAS THE GRAMOPHONE. A NEEDLE ON A HEAVY ARM SCRATCHED AT GROOVES ON A RECORD. THE MOST FAMOUS BRAND HAD THE TRADEMARK OF A DOG LISTENING TO HIS MASTER'S VOICE.

THIS GIVES ME THE NEEDLE!

THE FIRST TIME MOST PEOPLE IN THE UK LEARNED ABOUT CDs WAS IN 1981 ON A SCIENCE PROGRAMME. IT SAID YOU COULD SLAP JAM ON CDs AND THEY'D STILL PLAY*!

AND THIS IS THE SOUND OF THE BAND ERR... JAMMING!

GLOOP SLURP STICK

*THEY WON'T, SO DON'T!

MACHINES FOR PLAYING BACK MUSIC HAVE BECOME INSTRUMENTS THEMSELVES. DJs FOUND THAT HI-TECH TURNTABLES COULD BE STOPPED AND SPUN AGAIN AND STILL BE OK. THIS MEANT THEY COULD PLAY THE GROOVIEST BITS OF A RECORD AGAIN AND AGAIN AS IF THEY WERE ON A LOOP. THEY ALSO SCRATCHED THE NEEDLE ACROSS THE RECORDS TO MAKE CRAZY SOUNDS, TOO!

THAT'S LOOPY - BUT I LIKE IT!

I LIKE A GOOD SCRATCH MYSELF

ITCH

LATELY, THE INVENTION OF THE COMPRESSED DIGITAL MUSIC FILE HAS CHANGED THE WAY WE LISTEN TO AND BUY MUSIC.

compressed music file

PING

even more compressed music file

THANKS TO MP3 PLAYERS, MOBILE PHONES AND THE LIKE, ANYONE CAN MAKE AND PLAY MUSIC ANYWHERE... EVEN ON THE BUS!

NO SMOKING

SCREECH BLIP

THIS IS EVEN WORSE!!

PUZZLES

Name That Tune

We've put together the weirdest and wildest orchestra never seen, featuring the world's strangest musical instruments. But which instruments are real and which ones are a load of tuneless tripe?

OI!

1. **Whip** – a 'slap-stick' percussion instrument.

2. **Fatbutt** – a wide-bottomed 'wind' instrument.

3. **Sackbutt** – an early 'sacks-ophone'.

4. **Serpent** – a slippery wind instrument – very good for scales!

5. **Hurdy-gurdy** – a whining folk instrument played with a crank.

6. **Harmozium** – a squealing instrument with bellows – sounds like a strangled cat.

7. **Krazeechord** – electronic instrument featured on the theme tune to the TV series 'Dr Who'.

8. **Zither** – a Greek stringed instrument with a quiver-dithery sound.

9. **Kettle drum** – a drum filled with boiling water.

10. **Toaster drum** – a drum with pop-up drumskins.

11. **Lute** – like a flute, but with no 'F' note.

12. **Nose flute** – a flute played with the nose.

THIS ONLY PLAYS BUM NOTES!

cranky musician

cranky instrument

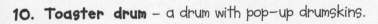

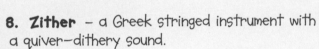

Sounds Ridiculous!

1. You can use sound to count the number of times a fly flaps its wings in a second.
TRUE/FALSE

2. You can hear sounds more quickly on a hot day.
TRUE/FALSE

3. If you lived in a lead box you wouldn't be able to hear any sounds from the outside.
TRUE/FALSE

4. You can listen to a concert underwater even if you're at the other end of the swimming pool.
TRUE/FALSE

BRAVO! GLUG!

Answers on page 60–61.

BAD GIG

It's a big moment for Micky Madness and the Rapid Rapping Crew – they're playing at Panic Park Festival. With everything wired up and ready, what can go wrong…?

1. It's a complicated business doing a live concert – you need lots of equipment and expertise. The most important piece of kit is the PA (Public Address) system. But how is it all connected up?

2. The instruments, including electric six-string (**2a**) and bass guitars (**2b**), have their own amplifiers (amps) and speakers (**2c**) which blast out the sound on stage. Microphones can be used to carry the sound of these small amps into the PA's bigger amp. The instruments can also be connected directly to small boxes called DI (Direct Injection) boxes (**2d**). They've got nothing to do with syringes – each box is used to 'inject' the sound from the instrument straight into the PA.

3. The sound from everything on stage is sent to the PA. This includes the DJ's turntables (**3a**) and the microphones on the drum kit (**3b**).

4. Somewhere – usually in the middle of the venue – an engineer mixes all the microphone and DI sounds together on a mixing desk. Each sound has its own set of controls – a channel. The idea is to make sure the audience can hear everything well – a good 'balance'. The result is blasted out of...

5. ...the large speakers at the front of the stage. Best not to get too close or you could go deaf! A 'roadie' (**5a**) – someone who goes on the road with the band, see? – is making sure no one gets caught in the cables.

6. These funny wedge-shaped speakers on stage are pointed at the band. The idea is that they will help the band hear themselves. One of the monitors (**6a**) has been damaged by an over–enthusiastic break–dancer (**6b**)! Another mixing desk, this time on stage (**6c**), is used to make sure that everyone in the band can hear what they need to.

7. This rapper's microphone isn't working. She and the other vocalists are using 'wireless' radio microphones, which, through transmitters on their belts (**7a**), send a signal to the receiver (**7b**) on top of the PA. But the problem here is called 'breakthrough' – a clashing of frequencies when two mikes transmit at the same wavelength.

8. What's going on here? Another radio wave mix–up means a radio station is coming through the guitar amp. Now that's bad news!

9. The screech coming out of the speaker is called feedback. This occurs when a microphone is too close to a speaker. The mike picks up the speaker sound which gets sent through the amplifier again and again until it gets horribly loud and makes a screechy noise. A lot like Micky Madness, then!

MAKE WAVES

So - sound is vibrations. If you make different lengths of vibrations, you get different notes. Here's a simple and watery way to make an instrument. The notes are made by creating different lengths of columns of air...

HORRIBLE HEALTH WARNING

You MUST ask permission before using any glasses, as your parents may not think it's such a 'smashing' idea if they get broken.

1 Use your ruler and make a mark on the side of the first glass or jar with your pen, at a height of about 12cm.

2 Now do the same with the other two, at heights of 10cm and 8cm. Fill each one with water up to the mark on its side

SPLOSH!

No.1 top dog

3 Write the numbers 1, 2 and 3 on your stickers and stick them on the glasses – number 1 goes on the glass holding the most water, down to 3 on the least full.

HOWL!

PLONK! PLONK!

PLINK! PLINK!

3212333 222 333
3212333 322321

4 You're now ready to play a tune! Take your pencil and GENTLY tap the glasses near the top, in the order of numbers in the splat above. Can you guess what the tune is?

Blowing in the Wind

Now let's test how wind instruments work.

You will need:
- two glass bottles
- air from your lungs
- a pair of lips (preferably your own)

1 Fill each bottle with water – up to about half full for one and a quarter full for the other.

2 Place your bottom lip on the rim of the first bottle and blow gently across the top. Do the same with the second bottle. They should make a different sound.

See Sound Waves

If you still don't believe that sound is just vibrations, look no further.

You will need:
- a mixing bowl
- cling film
- an elastic band (optional)
- salt
- an old saucepan
- a large wooden spoon

2 Sprinkle salt on top of the cling film.

1 Stretch cling film across the open top of the bowl and pull it as tight as you can until it's smooth all over. Put an elastic band around the rim to keep it in place.

3 Now hold the saucepan upside down near the bowl and bang the bottom with the spoon to create a short, sharp sound. The salt should leap up in the air. Clapping your hands or shouting will work too.

35

DAZZLING IDEAS

Okay, so trying to understand light can be blindingly
bewildering, but you really don't need to be brilliant to get light right.
Read on, bright sparks…

FOR CENTURIES THE QUESTION OF JUST EXACTLY WHAT LIGHT WAS MADE OF — WAVES OR PARTICLES? — HUNG AROUND LIKE A BOGEY FROM A SCIENCE TEACHER'S NOSE…

DO YOU MIND?!

THE QUESTION IS HARDER TO CRACK THAN A DRIED PEA FROM LAST TERM'S SCHOOL DINNER.

AND THAT'S HARD!

AND AS FOR THE FACTS — THEY'RE HARDER TO UNTANGLE THAN A VAT OF SPAGHETTI.

IS IT A LITTLE WAVE, LIKE THIS?

WHAT'S A LIGHT WAVE?

STUPID BOY — LIGHT TRAVELS IN WAVES!

IF YOU ASK A SCIENTIST TO EXPLAIN ABOUT LIGHT IT'S EVEN WORSE. YOU'RE BOUND TO GET AN ANSWER WITH LOTS OF FRIGHTENINGLY COMPLICATED SCIENTIFIC WORDS…

WHY IS THE SKY BLUE?

THE VISIBLE ELECTROMAGNETIC WAVELENGTH IS DUE TO THE RANDOM DEVIATION OF PHOTONS BY ATOMIC PARTICLES. IT'S BLINDINGLY OBVIOUS…

WELL, LET'S SHINE SOME LIGHT ON THE SUBJECT THEN. FIRSTLY, ALL THE LIGHT WE CAN SEE* COMES FROM THE SUN AND HOT GLOWING OBJECTS.

OI, WHAT ABOUT US GLOWING BEASTS?

ALL RIGHT, MR DEEP SEA GRUMP, KEEP YOUR SCALES ON. SOME TYPES OF LIGHT DON'T INVOLVE HEAT. THEY INCLUDE EERIE GLOWING CREATURES AND CHEMICALS THAT SHINE IN THE DARK.

*Waves of light energy aren't always visible to the naked eye!
How's that for a blinding fact?

36

IN 1901 THE SCIENTIST MAX PLANCK GOT IT SPOT ON. USING MATHS, PLANCK EXPLAINED HOW LIGHT CAN BE TURNED INTO HEAT INSIDE A BLACK BOX.

LIGHT!

SIR, WHAT'S IN THE BOX?

SO IT'S NOT BLACK IN THERE THEN?

PLEASE, TRY TO THINK OUTSIDE THE BOX!

BUT YOU SAID THINK ABOUT WHAT'S IN THE BOX!

THE ONLY WAY HIS CALCULATIONS ADDED UP WERE IF THE LIGHT CAME IN BLIPS OF ENERGY CALLED 'QUANTA'.

THESE DAYS ENERGY QUANTA ARE CALLED PHOTONS.

YOU LOOK DAZZLING MR QUANTA...

LET ME TAKE THIS OPPORTUNITY TO ANNOUNCE MY NEW NAME — PHOTON!

STAGE DOOR

IT'S A PHOTON OPPORTUNITY!

BEAM ME UP!

IT TOOK A YOUNG BRAINBOX CALLED ALBERT EINSTEIN TO PROVE PLANCK RIGHT. EINSTEIN GOT INTERESTED IN LIGHT AT THE AGE OF 14. HE WOULD DAYDREAM THAT HE WAS RIDING ON TOP OF A BEAM OF LIGHT IN SPACE.

HIS THEORIES EXPLAINED HOW PHOTONS ZIP AROUND SO FAST THEY BECOME WAVES.

WAVES! GOOD IDEA! THE PHOTONS MOVE SO FAST THAT THEY FORM WAVES!

COOOOEEEH! ALBERT!

ALBERT'S THEORIES ALSO SUGGESTED THAT LIGHT COULD BE BENT BY GRAVITY. GALAXIES AND SUNS BEND LIGHT WITH THEIR MASSIVE GRAVITATIONAL PULL.

BUT I THOUGHT LIGHT TRAVELLED IN STRAIGHT LINES!

SPACE

LIGHT

YES, BUT SOMETIMES THOSE STRAIGHT LINES ARE BENT!

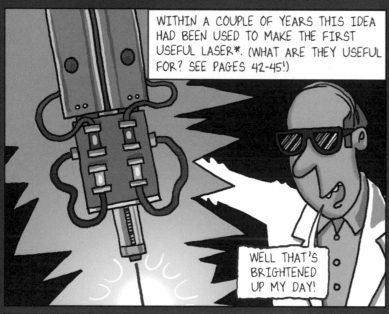

* Laser is short for Light Amplification by Stimulated Emission of Radiation

BEND A BEAM

Light travels in straight lines, right? Well, yes, but there are ways of making it change direction, as this loony experiment will show.

1 Wrap some kitchen foil around the end of a small bright torch, with the shiniest side facing the torch. Hold the foil in place with an elastic band. Using the point of a pencil, make a 2mm-wide hole in the centre of the foil.

2 Take a square-sided jar or bottle and fill it 9cm high with water. Then add a splash of milk and stir. The water should be very slightly cloudy, but still see-through.

3 Now shine the light up so it hits the underside of the water. What do you notice? Does the light seem to flicker like a dodgy TV? Does it dance sideways? Or does the light seem to bounce down at an angle?

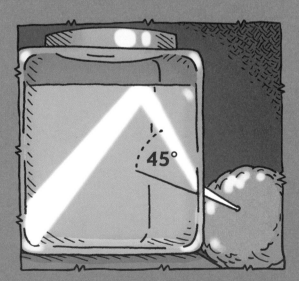

4 Now place the torch about 5cm away from the side of the jar. Try shining the light up or down from different angles.

5 You should see that from some angles the light beam jumps to one side as it passes through the sides of the jar.

39

NIGHT LIGHTS

So we can stay safe and see where we're going at night, there are many sources of light in towns. Some reflect it back, and others give off crazy colours.

1. Ordinary 'incandescent' light bulbs are glass bulbs filled with either an 'inert' gas such as argon (inert means it won't react with other elements) or a vacuum. Inside, a tungsten filament glows white-hot when electricity pulses through it.

2. Low pressure sodium vapour lamps are brighter yet use less power than most. Their orange-yellow colour is restful on night-driving eyeballs. High pressure sodium lights illuminate the church (**2a**).

3. Vehicle headlights are mosty the halogen type. Inside, the lamp has reflective mirrors (**3a**) to focus a low, wide beam that doesn't dazzle other motorists. Super-bright halogen light comes from a very hot tungsten filament in a halogen gas—filled quartz envelope. (A glass case would melt.) Police cars have eye-catching flashing halogen lights (**3b**) and a bungling burglar is caught by a movement—triggered halogen security light (**3c**).

4. The police car is nabbed by a speed camera. Its flashbulb zaps twice so the distance travelled over a set time (speed) is recorded on film. Oops!

5. An oil spill reflects a rainbow of shimmering colours ('iridescence'). Road signs also have a reflective surface so they appear to light up in vehicle headlights.

6. A mobile phone has a liquid crystal display (LCD), like a flat—screen TV. A grid of special crystals lets light pass through when a current is applied.

7. Light emitting diodes (LEDs), for bike lights and fun decoration (**7a**), are bright, use little electricity and burn for ages.

8. Mercury vapour lamps in a watertight case are great for underwater displays. Reflraction in the water (**8a**) makes distorted effects.

9. A mirror reflects your ugly mug when you peer at it!

10. Neon gas discharge lamps have various shapes and vivid colours – great for advertising signs.

11. The eyes of foxes (like those of cats (**11a**), dogs, dolphins, rats and whales) are reflective for maximum sensitivity in dim light. As light passes through the retina, a membrane behind bounces it back for a second pass.

LIGHT WORKS

Lasers are an amazing way of using light energy in incredibly accurate ways. They can be more useful than a calculator in a maths lesson…

Lasers are super-concentrated beams of fizzing photons. Lasers can do many amazing things. In fact, lasers make light work of many jobs…

1 Laser beams read barcodes in shops, libraries and so on. Take a look at the back of this book. Can you see a white rectangle with a pattern of black lines? The pattern is a unique code for this annual. You may have seen a supermarket checkout person passing each item across a scanner. A laser beam in the scanner flickers as it picks up the lines and the beam is read by a computer that recognizes the code from the pattern of flickers. You could say it's an idea that's really along the right lines.

2 Lasers can be life-savers. They can cut through human flesh and seal the edges of a wound as they do so, so you won't get much bleeding. By firing a laser down an endoscope (that's a tube containing optical fibres) you can perform life-saving operations deep within the body. A laser can even weld back a retina that has come adrift from the inside of an eyeball.

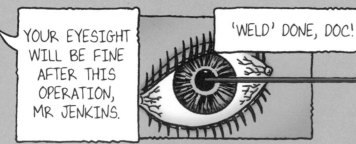

YOUR EYESIGHT WILL BE FINE AFTER THIS OPERATION, MR JENKINS.

'WELD' DONE, DOC!

3 A laser beam makes a snappy snipper! Lasers are used in factories to cut fabric at 15 metres per second.

4 A laser beam 'reads' a CD or DVD by flickering as it reflects off a pattern of pits on its surface. The player turns this flickering light signal into electrical pulses and then into your fave music.

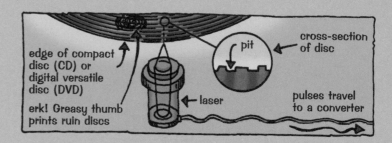

edge of compact disc (CD) or digital versatile disc (DVD)

erk! Greasy thumb prints ruin discs

← laser

pit

cross-section of disc

pulses travel to a converter

5 Laser beams can be used to liven up boring pop concerts. Simply fire the laser into the air and wave it around to make dramatic light patterns. Who cares if the music's rubbish? (Erm, we do!)

GREAT LASERS…

YEAH, BUT I'M GLAD WE BROUGHT OUR OWN MUSIC!

6 Laser beams travel in straight lines so you can use them as super-precise rulers. Your dad may even have a laser measurer – better than a floppy old tape measure! Lasers can also help to build straight tunnels. Simply fire a beam from the entrance of the tunnel and get digging along the line of the beam. Lasers were used this way to help dig the Channel Tunnel that links France and England.

7 A laser beam can melt and weld metals. And unlike any other tool a laser beam never becomes blunt from use.

8 Lasers can measure tiny earthquakes. Lasers on the San Andreas Fault in California, USA are linked up to monitoring equipment. Any wobbles in the light beam that are caused by the tiniest tremors in the ground can be detected instantly.

SORRY, THAT TREMOR WAS MY FAULT – WE HAD BAKED BEAN STEW FOR TEA LAST NIGHT

9 Laser printers work by firing an image of the page you're printing on to a light-sensitive drum. This drum has an electrical force which then picks up toner (the coloured stuff) and prints on the paper. Laser printers are fast – maybe that's because they keep in toner – ha ha.

But that's just the start of what lasers can do. They're so useful that scientists have really taken a shine to them!

Speedy signals

Don't forget that light is FAST with a capital F. And so is laser light.

• In just 0.14 seconds you can send a laser signal all around the world.

OUCH! I TOLD YOU TO POINT THAT LASER AWAY FROM ME!

I DID BUT IT WENT ROUND THE WORLD AND SHOT YOU IN THE BUM

• In 2.5 seconds you can send a light signal to the Moon and back again. In the 1960s US scientists did this. By timing the signal they were able to calculate the exact distance of the Moon from Earth.

• A laser could send a light signal to Mars in just three minutes. (The Martians' reply would take another three minutes.)

THIS IS PLANET EARTH... IS THERE ANYTHING TO EAT ON YOUR WORLD?

3 MINUTES

YES, EARTHLINGS – MARZ BARS, MARZIPAN AND MARTIAN MALLOWS

But laser signals aren't just for chatting with aliens. You probably use them every time you pick up a phone.

Listening lasers

When you talk into a phone connected to a fibre optic cable, the technology that turns laser light into sound in a CD works in reverse.

electric pulses are converted into light pulses

light pulses bounce off the fibre's inside surface until it reaches the other end

OUR VOICES ARE CONVERTED INTO LIGHT SIGNALS, MILDRED!

one fibre optic cable can hold thousands of fibres

light pulses are converted back into electric pulses

YOU DO TALK NONSENSE, BETTY. THAT WOULD NEVER WORK!

A microphone turns the sound of your voice into electrical pulses which are transformed into laser light signals. At the other end of the line the process is reversed and you can hear the sound. Because light moves so fast and lasers can flicker at billions of times a second, an optical fibre carries a conversation down the line in the blink of an eye. And what's more, you can squash thousands of fibres into a single cable.

LASER DAYS

It's a sunny day in the local park. Whether folks are frolicking or just soaking up some rays, light plays a part in their fun. And whatever day of the week it is, when it comes to light in the park, it's always a 'sun day'!

1. Our Sun is the biggest light source around. Sensible people use solar panels (**1a**) to turn its rays into electrical energy.

2. The Sun's rays include the whole range of light – from infrared (IR) to ultraviolet (UV).

3. Those UV rays can damage unprotected skin. They can cause skin cancers by mucking up the skin's DNA, so slip something on or slap on some suncream!

4. Bright sunlight can be dazzling and hurt your eyes. That's why bright people wear polarizing sunglasses. These are basically polarizing filters. (Many car windscreens are the same.) The filters work by letting in only one plane (direction of wave movement) of light (**4a**). Some sunglasses cut out UV rays, too.

5. UV rays can be dead useful... Some flykillers use them to attract flies then zap 'em dead!

6. Some silly people sit under UV lamps to top up their tan. Trouble is, this makes Sun damage much more likely. (Plus their skin can eventually end up looking all leathery!)

7. Many lasers work hard while we laze around! DVD and CD players use them to read the microscopic pits of digital info on the discs (**7a**).

8. The accuracy of lasers means they can be used for incredibly delicate operations such as eye surgery. And because lasers make perfect straight lines, surveyors use laser 'theodolites' – instruments for measuring angles – (**8a**) to make perfect measurements of roads and other places.

9. Lasers can be used for less important stuff, too – such as zapping the roots of hairs on hairy legs! This is similar to electrolysis. The lasers act like tiny hot needles, burning the roots of the hairs. Ouch!

10. Some road markings soak up sunlight during the day, and give it off as a glow at night.

11. Light is also used to send superfast signals down amazing 'fibre optic' cables.

12. Meanwhile, nature gets on with turning the Sun's energy into food energy by photosynthesis. It's the original 'green' idea!

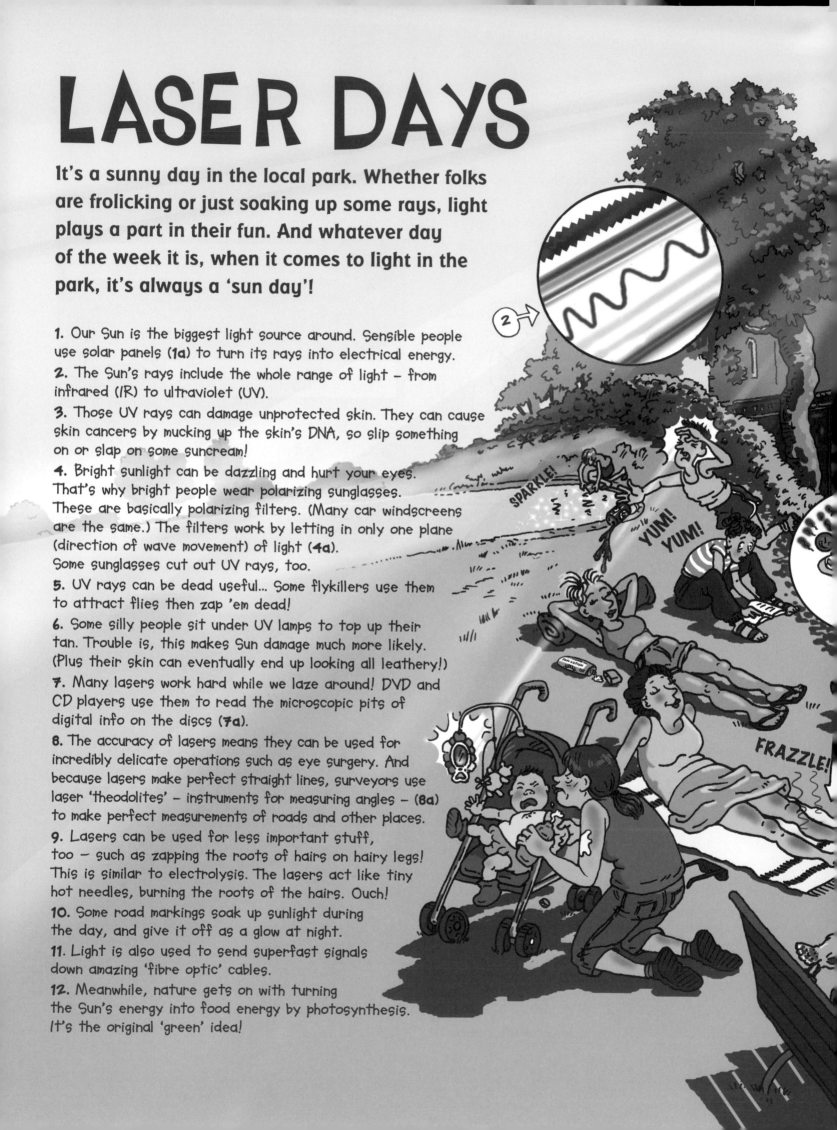

PUZZLES

FRIGHTENING LIGHT QUIZ

Shine a light on these statements, please, and decide whether they are right about light or darkly false...

1. Without sunlight you can't see a rainbow. TRUE/FALSE

2. Without sunlight you can't see the Moon. TRUE/FALSE

3. If it's completely dark your face won't appear in a mirror. TRUE/FALSE

4. If it's totally dark you can't take holiday snaps. TRUE/FALSE

5. In the dark, a poisonous rattlesnake couldn't find where you are hiding. TRUE/FALSE

FAZED BY LASERS?
Lasers are used in an amazing variety of equipment. But which of the tools and toys in lab assistant Jim Dim's room use lasers?

Answers on page 61.

LOOPY LEARNING

Learning is a vital part of life. We learn with our brains, bodies, five senses and even with our emotions, both at school and elsewhere. To explain more about the ups and downs of understanding, we brought in a learned friend, Professor Potter.

HELLO, CHILDREN. I'M PROFESSOR POTTER, HERE TO TELL YOU ABOUT HOW WE LEARN THINGS – AND WE DON'T JUST LEARN FROM SCHOOLWORK! YOU NEVER STOP LEARNING IN LIFE, EVEN WHEN YOU'RE A WISE OLD OWL LIKE ME!

HE'S POTTY

TWIT!

FROM NURSERY SCHOOL, YOU LEARN ALL SORTS OF SKILLS, SOMETIMES WITHOUT REALIZING IT. BROADLY SPEAKING, THESE ARE MENTAL, PHYSICAL AND EMOTIONAL SKILLS. BUT NOT EVERYONE LEARNS AT THE SAME PACE!

WAAHHH

SMASH

CRAM

CUDDLE

CHILDREN LEARN NEW WORDS AT A PHENOMENAL RATE. FROM THE AGE OF ONE, THAT'S AROUND TEN WORDS A DAY! BUT THAT'S NOT TO SAY THEY ALWAYS UNDERSTAND THEM!

SO WHAT WORDS HAVE YOU LEARNT TODAY?

TOTAL GA-GA!

MOST LEARNING METHODS INVOLVE SOMETHING CALLED COGNITION. THIS ISN'T ANYTHING TO DO WITH COGS, BUT IS ALL ABOUT HOW YOUR BRAIN TAKES IN AND USES INFORMATION.

WHAT WAS THAT? I THINK I'M GOING...

...CUCKOO!

MEMORIZING THINGS IS THE FIRST FORM OF COGNITIVE LEARNING. IN SCHOOL THIS IS SOMETIMES DONE 'PARROT FASHION', BY REPEATING YOUR MULTIPLICATION TABLES ALOUD.

...IS COMPREHENSION (UNDERSTANDING) OF WHAT YOU'VE LEARNT, THEN ANALYSIS (SEPARATING THE DIFFERENT PARTS). YOU USE THESE MENTAL SKILLS WHEN FOLLOWING THE INSTRUCTIONS TO ASSEMBLE A TOY AEROPLANE KIT, FOR EXAMPLE.

BUT REPEATING THINGS OVER AND OVER DOESN'T HELP YOU UNDERSTAND THEM. SO THE NEXT STAGE...

WHEN YOU'VE UNDERSTOOD THE INSTRUCTIONS AND IDENTIFIED ALL THE PARTS, PUTTING IT ALL TOGETHER IS CALLED SYNTHESIS. IT'S NOT ALWAYS EASY!

THE FINAL COGNITIVE STAGE IS CALLED EVALUATION, WHERE YOU MAKE A DECISION BASED ON ALL THE OTHER STAGES. JUDGES USE THIS IN COURT, AS DO FOOTBALL MANAGERS TO DECIDE PLAYERS' BEST POSITIONS.

OF COURSE, WE LEARN PHYSICAL SKILLS TOO, PRACTISING MOVEMENTS THAT INVOLVE HAND AND EYE COORDINATION. THIS MIGHT INVOLVE PLAYING BEAUTIFUL MUSIC...

...OR DRIVING A CAR.

I SAID LEFT, RIGHT!

EFFECTIVE LEARNING IS ALL ABOUT UNDERSTANDING EMOTIONS. THAT OFTEN MEANS UNDERSTANDING YOURSELF, AND HOW TO BEHAVE TOWARDS OTHERS. SOMETIMES THAT MEANS HIDING YOUR FEELINGS...

THANK YOU GRANNY, THAT'S ER- LOVELY!

BUT AFTER LOTS OF PRACTICE, YOU CAN USE THESE SKILLS MORE NATURALLY, IMPROVISE IN ALL SITUATIONS AND MAKE MORE COMPLEX MANOEUVRES.

TINKLE

LEFT HAND DOWN A BIT

THAT'S A GOOD IDEA!

BEEP   BEEP   BEEP

...AT OTHER TIMES IT MEANS NOT HIDING EMOTIONS AT ALL!

HOME   AWA
0 - 4

GOING THROUGH ALL THESE LEARNING STAGES AND ADDING LOTS OF EXPERIENCE EVENTUALLY LEADS TO GREAT WISDOM. AT LEAST IN THEORY...

SPLOSH

MORE TEA, MOTHER?

NOW SEE MORE LEARNING LUNATICS AND BAFFLING BRAINBOXES ON THE NEXT PAGES...

BRAIN GAMES

The brain learns just like someone playing a computer game for the first time, figuring out the new skills needed for each increasingly difficult level…

1. Why do grown ups talk like this to their babies? Well, they're helping the baby's brain get used to the basic sounds of speech. (Still sounds stupid though!)

2. When a baby pays attention, the memory and recognition functions in the brain step up a gear. The hippocampus (**2a**) sends signals through the brain, making new connections – synapses – between neurons. In the synapses, receptors hook up with calcium (**2b**) to make connections easier the next time.

3. Flashing lights and fast music stimulate the senses, triggering the release of dopamine in the brain and the adrenal system, making the brain feel excited and happy!

4. Training your brain to get your limbs to do exactly what you want – coordination – takes a while to learn. This is why toddlers get really frustrated when they drop stuff or can't reach them. It must be as irritating – or rewarding – as one of these tricky toy-grabbing machines.

5. Your parents might disagree, but video games improve skills of recognition, problem–solving and patience – 'cognitive skills'.

6. When someone tries a tricky problem for the first time, their brain gets bamboozled and has to use more energy. This is true for gamers. New players' brains use more energy than those of experts. Scientists discovered this by tracking the glucose levels in players' brains (**6a**).

7. Older brains don't just wither away. They still make new neurons at the age of 70. That means memories can be kept up and new skills CAN be learnt. You CAN teach your grandma to destroy alien zombie attackers!

8. Learning to dance on command is an awesome skill. But some brains never learn. This brain should know not to eat a hot-dog and an extra large coke before going on a disco challenge!

9. The more a brain does a certain activity, the easier it finds it. With practice, brains can do several tasks at the same time without too much trouble. For example, your dad can drive and talk at the same time… unfortunately!

BATTY GREY MATTER

Time to relax and switch off from all that learning and have some ice cream and jelly. But oh dear, it seems even those delights can stress your poor brainbox!

ICE CREAM HEADACHE

Eating an ice cream can cause a nasty headache. If the ice cream touches the roof of your mouth it shocks the nerves that lead to your baffled brainbox. A headache is a brain pain. When you're under stress, more blood squirts into your brain.

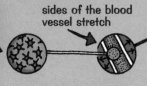

tiny blobs in your blood called platelets pile into your brain's narrow blood vessels

sides of the blood vessel stretch

The best thing to do if the ice cream brings on a headache is to touch the roof of your mouth with your nice warm tongue. This relaxes the nerves.

ARGH!

ice cream

Alternatively, you could let the ice cream melt a bit before stuffing your little face.

NO WAY!

But something you shouldn't do when you've got a headache is frown with the pain. By frowning, you squeeze kilometres of blood vessels in your head. This squashes the blood platelets and makes the pain more intense. The best thing to do with a headache is to relax and try to feel happy. When you smile the blood vessels relax and your headache should ease.

RELIGIOUS RECITAL

Children at school have to learn an average of ten new words every day, but that's nothing! Bhanddanta Vicittabi Vumsa of Burma learnt and recited 16,000 pages of Buddhist text off by heart.

PAGE 14,763 IS FASCINATING...

MEMORY LOSS

Car crashes are never good news for your beastly body, but your brainbox is especially vulnerable to harm. The effect of the brain being jolted forwards is even more damaging than a blow to the head. The shock can tear blood vessels and the brain itself, leaving wounds that cannot easily be treated because they're inside the skull.

The effects of an injury can depend on which part of the brain gets damaged. It can lead to problems reading, smelling or tasting. It can also cause a condition called amnesia – that's loss of memory, remember?

THANKS – WHO ARE YOU?

25th WEDDING

BRAINBOX BAFFLERS

Illusions are freaky and great fun! But why and how do they work? Do our eyes lie or do our brains come up with balderdash? Let's find out – with the help of an all-seeing alien with a hard drive for a head…

EVER THOUGHT YOUR MIND WAS PLAYING TRICKS ON YOU?

EXCELLENT WORK – YOU GOT 100%... RELAX AND HAVE FUN FOR THE REST OF THE DAY!

EH? DOES NOT COMPUTE!

A+

...OR BEEN ON A TRAIN AND THOUGHT YOU WERE MOVING WHEN ACTUALLY YOU WERE LOOKING AT A TRAIN ON THE NEXT LINE MOVING ALONGSIDE?

MIND THE GAP!

NO SMOKING

ARE YOU ALL RIGHT, DEAR?

I'M GOING OFF THE RAILS!

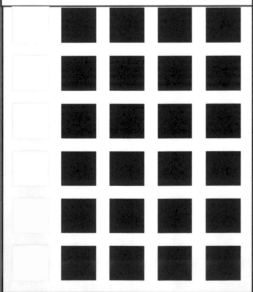

SOME ILLUSIONS ARE DELIBERATELY DESIGNED TO CREATE THAT STATE OF CONFUSION IN YOUR MIND. DO YOU SEE GREY SPOTS BETWEEN THESE SQUARES?

THERE AREN'T ANY! IN YOUR EYES, RECEPTOR CELLS WHICH SEE THE WHITE BITS BETWEEN THE SQUARES ARE BEING BULLIED – 'INHIBITED' – BY THE ONES RECEIVING THE BLACK.

OI, STOP BULLYING – WE CAN'T SEE THE WHITE BITS!

OTHER ILLUSIONS BOGGLE YOUR MIND BY NOT GIVING IT ENOUGH INFO TO DECIDE WHAT IT'S SEEING... IS THIS A DUCK OR A RABBIT?

QUACK

SNIFF

I DON'T KNOW WHETHER TO GIVE IT BREAD OR A CARROT!

WHAT HAPPENS WHEN YOU SPOT THIS DOTTY PICTURE?

THE DOTS ARE TURNED INTO A PATTERN WHICH IS SENT TO YOUR VISUAL CORTEX. THE CORTEX PASSES IT ON TO A CLEVERER LEVEL OF BRAIN THAT RECOGNIZES SHAPE. AND FINALLY, A TOP-LEVEL BRAIN ZONE SUSSES THE SPECIES.

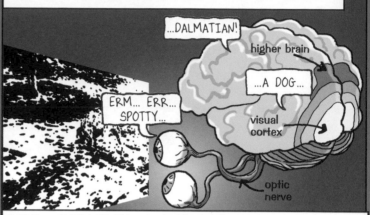

...DALMATIAN!

higher brain

...A DOG...

ERM... ERR... SPOTTY...

visual cortex

optic nerve

THERE ARE TEN TIMES AS MANY CONNECTIONS GOING BACK THE OTHER WAY, FROM THE 'HIGHER' BRAIN TO THE BOTTOM.

IT'S ALMOST AS IF YOUR TOP BRAIN IS A BOSSY BOOTS.

NO, NO, IT'S A DALMATIAN!

BUT THEY'RE ONLY SPOTS!

ONCE THE TOP BRAIN HAS MADE UP ITS MIND THEN THAT'S WHAT YOU SEE. HORRIBLE SCIENCE TECHNICAL TERM ALERT: THIS IS CALLED TOP-DOWN PROCESSING.

MAGICIANS MAKE USE OF THE BOSSINESS OF YOUR UPPER BONCE. IF THEY CAN CONVINCE IT SOMETHING'S HAPPENING, YOU WILL SEE IT HAPPEN – EVEN THOUGH YOU KNOW IT'S IMPOSSIBLE.

SAW SAW

MY HIGHER BRAIN IS TELLING ME IT'S ALL FINE...

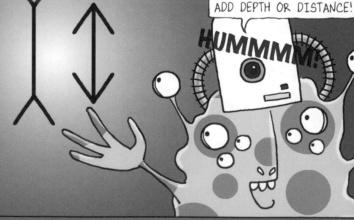

TO AVOID BEING CONFUSED BY ALL THESE ILLUSIONS YOU'D HAVE TO BE A SUPER ALIEN WITH ULTRA ALL-SEEING EYES... AND A 'BOTTOM-UP' PROCESSING COMPUTER THAT TAKES MORE NOTICE OF WHAT IT SEES THAN WHAT IT KNOWS.

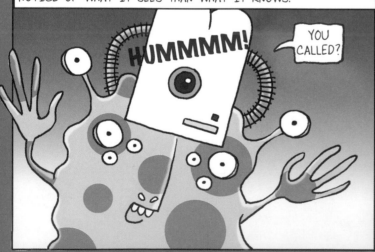

HUMMMM!

YOU CALLED?

IN THIS FAMOUS STICK DRAWING ILLUSION, WHICH VERTICAL LINE IS LONGER?

THEY ARE THE SAME LENGTH! YOUR WEAK HUMAN HIGHER MIND IS CONFUSED BY THE ARROWS, THINKING THEY ADD DEPTH OR DISTANCE!

HUMMMM!

EVEN ROOMS CAN BE MADE TO MESS WITH YOUR MIND. 'AMES ROOMS' USE OPTICAL ILLUSIONS TO MAKE YOU LOOK TEENSY WHEN YOU STAND IN ONE PART OF THE ROOM AND HUGE WHEN YOU WALK TO ANOTHER.

THIS IS IMPOSSIBLE, BUT I LIKE IT!

THE THING IS, TRICKING YOUR BONCE CAN BE FUN!

IT'S NOT IMPOSSIBLE TO DRAW - YOUR MIND IS FOOLED BY PARALLEL LINES HAVING UNEXPECTED ENDINGS AND JOINS!

WITHOUT ILLUSIONS, PAINTINGS WOULDN'T BE SO LOVELY. 'PERSPECTIVE' - SHOWING THINGS THAT ARE FARTHER AWAY AS SMALLER - IS A WAY OF CREATING AN ILLUSION OF DEPTH ON A FLAT SURFACE.

WHAT A LOVELY LANDSCAPE!

RUBBISH! THAT'S NOT A LANDSCAPE, IT'S OIL PAINT ON A FLAT CANVAS!

HYPNOSIS IS A HANDY BIT OF MIND MAGIC WHICH SEEMS TO WORK BY GETTING YOUR TOP BRAIN TO GO INTO A DIFFERENT STATE - SO ALL THE USUAL SENSORY STUFF IS OVERRULED. COULD BE USEFUL FOR EATING SCHOOL DINNERS!

I AM OVERRIDING MY SENSORY INFORMATION SO I CAN EAT MY CABBAGE. YUM, IT IS LOVELY!

HUMMMM!

NO IT'S NOT, IT'S GROSS!

BUT THERE ARE SOME THINGS THAT MIGHT BAFFLE EVEN THE MOST ADVANCED ILLUSION-PROOF COMPUTER-BRAIN...

DAD MUM

YES DEAR, I DO FIND YOUR FATHER ATTRACTIVE!

GAK

DOES NOT COMPUTE!

BZZZZ

MIRAGE MANSION

Welcome to the freaky home of TV illusionist and magician Saul N Illusion.
Have a look around – but beware: not everything is what it seems...

1. See the advertisement painted on the pitch of the cricket ground next to Saul's home? It looks distorted and odd when viewed from player level. But when seen from a high-up camera on TV **(1a)** the ad appears to stand upright, making it hard to ignore. That's not cricket!

2. While one boy watches from this tree, another climber stares through the branches at the lake in the distance. Look at branches with moving water behind them **(2a)** and they appear to go a bit wibbly, as if they're moving too.

3. Saul's son can see faces in the clouds. Ever noticed the way you can't quite make out cloud faces at first, then they become obvious **(3a)**? This shows you how the higher brain takes over, imposing patterns or shapes that aren't actually there.

4. A van packed with the tools of Saul's trade.

5. Saul is trying to give up smoking. Luckily, he can use his own self-hypnosis recordings **(5a)**!

6. Two old fogeys in the loft – or is one of them someone playing guitar? It's actually an old-fashioned illusion from Saul's collection.

7. From a distance, heat haze on tarmac looks like a pool of water, thanks to the way hot air reflects and bends light. This is known as a mirage.

8. When you watch TV, your brain perceives the rapid sequence of images as movement. Dogs just see flickering. Must be really confusing for Saul's dog – he can hear his master's voice coming from that box!

9. This phrenology head bust is a relic of the non-science of brain bumps.

10. Painted on the back wall is a 'trompe l'oeil' (say 'tromp loy'. It's French for 'trick the eye'). It's a realistic painting of a lovely view from a window where there's actually just a wall.

11. A cricketer drinks from a fountain which seems to be both level with him and behind him. The base of the balcony **(11a)** and the step-seat **(11b)** don't make sense, either! Well, this is the house of Saul N Illusion... 's all an illusion... geddit??! Spot more oddities in the picture in Saul's room and the trees!

MAKE A FREAKY FACE

The brain is divided into two halves, joined in the middle. The left side generally deals with facts and calculations and the right with feelings and artistic, touchy-feely stuff. Let's see if we can baffle it with back-to-front and upside-down horrors!

HORRIBLE HEALTH WARNING!
MAKE SURE YOU GET AN ADULT TO HELP WITH THE PANEL MARKED WITH THIS SIGN.

You will need:
- a big photo of a face (ideally yours)
- a small rectangular mirror, such as one from a make-up kit
- scissors
- glue
- a sheet of paper
- a friend

1 Find a large mug-shot photo of yourself – or some other familiar face. You could cut one out of a magazine, so long as your mum isn't reading it at the time! If the face is small, make it bigger using a photocopier.

2 Place a small rectangular mirror lengthways over the photo of the face. Look at the right-hand side of the photo and its reflection in the mirror, which completes the image. The face should look strange and a bit scary.

3 Now take the photo and use scissors to carefully cut out the eyes and the mouth. (Ask an adult to help you.)

4 Using glue, stick the photo on to a sheet of plain white paper. Then stick the eyes and the mouth in the proper places, but all upside down! The face should now look even more scary. Yikes!

5 Show it to your friend in stage 4 so she gets a fright – then tell her to look at it upside down. You may be surprised to find that your friend doesn't find this picture scary at all, and may even think it looks normal!

MAYBE EVEN BETTER THAN NORMAL!

SEE THROUGH YOUR HAND

Do your eyes ever play tricks on your poor old brainbox? This illusion will certainly throw it into horrible confusion...

1 Take a sheet of paper and roll it lengthways into a tube about 2cm in diameter.

ROLL

PEEP!

2 Hold the end of the tube close to your right eye and look through it. Now hold your left hand, palm flat and facing you, against the side of the tube and in front of your left eye.

3 With both eyes open, what do you see? It should appear as though you have a hole through your left hand. Move your left hand around a bit and the hole will move. Spooky!

PLATO'S CURSED TRIANGLE

Now here's a total brain boggler! Copy the triangle in picture A onto some graph paper. Now, if you swap the positions of the blue and red triangles, and move the yellow shape as shown in picture B, you'll be amazed and confused to see that one whole 'unit square' vanishes. How can this be?

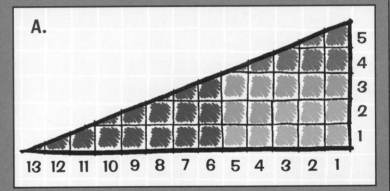

A.

5 4 3 2 1

13 12 11 10 9 8 7 6 5 4 3 2 1

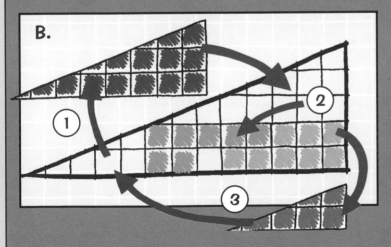

B.

① ② ③

C.

empty square ?

1. Move the red triangle to the top right.
2. Move the yellow shape left and down.

3. Move the blue triangle to the bottom left.
4. You are now left with one empty square!

Originally, the large outer triangle appeared to be EQUAL in area to the three coloured shapes. BUT, now the area of the outer triangle seems to be GREATER than the sum of those shapes. Can you work out what's happened? If you REALLY can't, then turn to page 61.

PUZZLE ANSWERS

So is your brain as sharp as a super-fast processor or as limp as a soggy spaghetti sandwich? Are you as bright as laser light or dim as a torch with flat batteries? There's only one way to find out...

GEIGER COUNTER p16

1. CLICK CLICK! Many smoke alarms use a tiny radioactive source. 2. Silence. 3. Silence. X-rays are made using a form of radiation... but aren't radioactive themselves. 4. CLICK CLICK! This 'isotope' of hydrogen is radioactive. 5. SILENCE. The Sun creates helium in fusion reactions, but helium is NOT usually radioactive. 6. CLICK! Some early pacemakers – heart regulating devices – used nuclear batteries. 7. CLICK CLICK CLICK! Yes, some parts of Cornwall have naturally occurring and dangerous levels of radon – a radioactive gas. 8. SILENCE. 9 SILENCE. Carbon-dating can be used to tell how old objects are, but the level of radiation measured is very low. 10. SILENCE. Well, none of these silences are actually totally quiet – Geiger counters ALWAYS click a little bit, because there is a harmlessly low level of radiation around us all the time.

WHICH SWITCH? p16

The correct switch is B.

EGG-SEPTIONAL p23

1. FALSE. Sometimes they are, but NOT always. 2. FALSE. Eggshell colour has nothing to do with the taste or the nutritional quality of an egg. 3. TRUE. Egg white contains no fat. 4. e) Any of these methods will kill bacteria that the egg may have picked up. 5. FALSE. You CAN buy pasteurized eggs, but most aren't pasteurized. 6. a) and b) A pong is a tell-tale sign that an egg is off. The pong is caused by the gas hydrogen sulfide, which is created when bacteria begins to break down the proteins in the egg white. If an egg does float, it's definitely off and too old to eat. But a cloudy white – c) – is just a sign that carbon dioxide hasn't had a chance to leave the egg, which actually means it's very fresh.

WHATEVER COULD IT BE? p23

It's... BANANA, of course.

BE A SCOFFIN' BOFFIN p23

1. b) The overweight people only ate more if the food was right in front of them. If the food wasn't in front of them, the thinner people ate more – because they went out and found it! 2. a) The people trying to lose weight were upset. The scientists told them the milk shake was fattening and that they had already broken their diet, so they pigged out on ice cream – they thought they might as well enjoy themselves.

DARE YOU DISCOVER... WHY SHELLS SOUND LIKE THE SEA? p27

2. Some of the sound is also made by the rush of warm air rising from your own hot, sweaty body. You can't normally hear this but the resonating shell makes it louder. (You can hear similar sounds if you cup your hand and place it over your ear.)

NAME THAT TUNE p31

1. REAL. Boringly, though, it's just two blocks which are slapped together. 2. FAKE. 3. REAL – actually a medieval wind instrument. There was plenty of wind around then. 4. REAL. 5. REAL. 6. FAKE. 7. FAKE. 8. REAL. 9. REAL, but it's not filled with boiling water. 10. FAKE. 11. REAL – but lutes are like guitars, not flutes. 12. REAL! Maybe players like to pick a tune on them?!

SOUNDS RIDICULOUS p31

1. TRUE. Scientists have found that a housefly's wings beat at 352 times per second. 2. TRUE. When air is warmer, its molecules have more energy and so move faster. Sound only travels about three per cent faster, so you will hardly notice the difference. 3. FALSE. Sounds pass easily through metal. 4. TRUE. Sounds travels well through water but your eardrums wouldn't work very well because of the water, so it would sound rather muffled.

BRAVO! GLUG!

FRIGHTENING LIGHT QUIZ p46

1. TRUE. A rainbow happens when sunlight shines through droplets of rain. This splits the sunlight into different colours. 2. TRUE. The Moon doesn't make its own light. That pretty silvery moonlight is sunlight reflected off the Moon.
3. TRUE. A mirror works by reflecting light. There's nothing to stop you looking at it in the dark, but since there's no light the mirror won't show your image. However, it's unusual for there to be no light at all in your house — you really need TOTAL darkness. Oh, and of course if you're a vampire your reflection won't show up at all. You're not a vampire, are you?!
4. FALSE. Especially if you use a flash. Even without the flash, many modern digital cameras have special settings that make the most of whatever tiny amount of light there is.
5. FALSE. A rattlesnake has a pit on each side of its head full of temperature sensors, which would detect the heat of your body. Yikes!

FAZED BY LASERS? p46

Three use lasers: 1. Laser microscopes provide amazing magnifications; 2. Tapeless tape measures use lasers to judge distances... and 3. Laser printers zap a laser at a roller to charge it with an image.

PLATO'S CURSED TRIANGLE p59

OK, brace your noggins! It's all down to the thickness of the outer line of the triangle. Look at it — it's thicker than a big brother. The thickness hides the fact that when the red and blue triangles are swapped, they move the top diagonal edge of the frame triangle outwards slightly, making it BIGGER. The amount it has grown equals one unit hence the new space! To check this: make a larger drawing and use a thin line instead of the thick one. Using the equation, 'The area of a triangle equals half the base times the height', you can calculate that the area of the outer triangle is 32.5 units. The yellow and green areas add up to 15. The red triangle appears to be 8 x 3 units — hence 12 units in area. The blue triangle appears to be 5 by 2 — hence 5 units in area. So 12+5 = 17 units. BUT... the illusion of the thick border hides the fact that the red triangle is wider than the 8 units it appears to be, and the blue triangle is taller than 2 units. Their combined area IS actually 17.5 units but appears to be only 17. When you switch their positions, they force the top diagonal edge out a bit, doubling the 0.5 difference — and so leaving a ONE unit hole. PHEW!!!! If you made it to the end of that lot, you truly are a Horrible Scientist!